Eltin Gr

Living Prayer

VERITAS

First published 1996 by
Veritas Publications
7-8 Lower Abbey Street
Dublin 1

Copyright © Eltin Griffin 1996

ISBN 1 85390 299 3

The numbers in parenthesis throughout the text refer to the paragraphs of the *Catechism of the Catholic Church*, copyright © (in Ireland) 1994 Veritas Publications – Libreria Editrice Vaticana. All rights reserved.

Cover design by Bill Bolger
Printed in Ireland by Paceprint Ltd, Dublin

'The more I know the more I don't know' is a saying that is particularly true of prayer. True for me anyway. I have been giving courses on prayer over the past three decades. I have been talking about prayer to a whole variety of groups in parishes, in retreat centres and in various mission fields. I have been illustrating at times how prayer might be carried out by the individual, by the family, by the small group and by the religious community. The well of discovery never seems to dry up. Each time I am asked to talk on prayer I discover aspects of the topic I had not realised before. The most precious insights have on occasion come from very ordinary people. I have been overwhelmed at times by a rare insight into a scripture text by a most unlikely individual. One can only pause and admit that one is walking on holy ground. I recall the well known story about the Curé d'Ars who asked the man from his parish what he was doing in the church during all the hours he spent there. The Curé himself was taken by surprise at the answer: 'He is looking at me and I am looking at him.'

The Catechism

The Catechism of the Catholic Church has opened new dimensions of prayer for me and even aspects of prayer I had long since forgotten. The Catechism is a very rich source of prayer and one that does not yield up its depths too easily. Like every human work it has its defects and omissions. The new Catechism is by its own admission an unfinished work, a point of reference for catechisms that will be composed in various countries and for adaptations of the content as required by differences of culture, age, spiritual maturity, social and ecclesial conditions (24). On the whole the Catechism can only be discussed as a treasure house of the Faith, a marvellous combination of the old and the new. The Catechism is a very important book for the life of the Church. A confrère of mine, a professional theologian, suggests one way of coming to grips with its rich contents. Read Book 4 first, the one on prayer, then 2, then 3, then 1. After we have read it fully we could dip into it again. After a few months we should read it again and then keep reading it. The Catechism does not make for light reading; it is after all, concerned with mysteries. We give thanks to God for this new gift to the Church.

Foundations

I am grateful to all who laid the foundations of prayer in my own life, to my parents, to my mother who imparted in her own way a lot of wisdom about prayer and to my father who seemed to be in touch with another world as he led the family Rosary. I am grateful to the teachers in the primary school in Cork City who encouraged us to learn prayer formulas by heart. Apart from the obvious ones we learned the

Memorare, the Magnificat, the Anima Christi (Soul of Christ) and the En Ego (Prayer before the Crucifix). How few children seem to know such formulas nowadays! Memorisation seems almost to be discouraged. Learning off formal prayers and bits of scripture serves to build up a Christian memory. What one learns in childhood leaves a lasting impression. The soldiers in the trenches of World War I went back to the prayers they had learned at their mother's knee, as the bombs were flying all around them. (2625)

Images

Images of the sacred will always have played a part when we recall the various stages in our life of prayer. Images can make for a big impression. I would love to see the birth of a decent form of art in the Christian home. The repository kind of art tends in the main to cheapen religion. Representing the Blessed Virgin Mary through the medium of plastic which one sees exhibited in piety shops at Marian shrines almost borders on the blasphemous. The Christians of the Orthodox East tend to have in their homes what they call an icon corner. Pride of place is given to the Lord himself, then to his Blessed Mother. The saints follow in stylised order. The local saint always finds a special place. The icons reveal a heavenly beauty enhanced by the lights for which the Orthodox have a particular fondness. As they go in and out of the house, they bless themselves and salute the icons.

Icons can promote visual prayer. An icon is a mirror which, by means of its quality of light, allows the Lord's glory to shine forth and draws the beholder inwards into the heart of mystery. Equally the icon becomes a window through which the unseen world looks through ours.

> And we with our unveiled faces reflecting like mirrors the brightness of the Lord all grow brighter and brighter as we are turned into the image [icon] that we reflect. This is the work of the Lord who is spirit. (2 Cor 3:18)

Icons are gradually finding a place in western homes. It is to be hoped that they are employed not just for their artistic value, which can be quite considerable. (2500-2502)

> The soul that has been totally enlightened by the indescribable beauty of Christ's face becomes wholly eye, wholly light, wholly face, wholly Spirit. (Macarius of Egypt)

Music

Music too can develop the spirit of prayer. Good music penetrates the crevices of the heart and makes for a very deep impression. The melody and the words can have a lasting effect. Augustine of Hippo puts it this way:

> How I wept, deeply moved by your hymns, songs and the voices that echoed through your church! What emotion I experienced in them!

Those sounds flowed into my ears distilling the truth in my heart. A feeling of devotion surged within me and tears streamed down my face – tears that did me good. (*Conf.* 9, 6, 14: PL 32, 769-770) (1157)

Sentimental hymns with banal language and impoverished theology serve only to reduce religion in the eyes of those who may be looking for stronger fare. There is a strength in good music which empowers the believer, whether it is the perennial chant, the Protestant inheritance of strong hymnody, the polyphonic rendering of a gem like the 'Ave Verum' or material of the quality that has come on stream with the vernacular liturgy such as Fintan O'Carroll's trumpet-like 'Alleluia'. A lot of dubious music has arrived from English-speaking countries which ill serves the liturgy and the spirit of prayer which the liturgy is intended to nourish. (1156-1158)

Young Christians

The language of prayer for many young Christians can be a strange one which fails to register. Their visual world tends to be one of posters of pop stars with which their bedroom walls are festooned. The sacred fails to find a place. The world which they inhabit is a world with a consumerist mentality, a world which invites to sensuality, to activism, to self-indulgence. There is a split between prayer and the rest of life. (2727)

On the other hand the official Church may sometimes fail to respond to the needs of young people in the area of the sacred by providing the tangible symbols and images which can have enormous drawing power when designed with both taste and sensitivity. The desire for God never completely dies away. There is a pattern in the scheme of things by which the sacred returns again in a new and invigorating form which leads to fresh enthusiasm. (2727)

Milan

What has happened in the Diocese of Milan under the leadership of Cardinal Martini shows what enlightened leadership can attain. Martini had no great belief in large assemblies in church before he arrived in Milan. He proved himself wrong. From talking with a small group of young people on the lawn of his residence about the Word of God he arrived at a stage where he found himself addressing five thousand young people in the cathedral. There was singing, reading of the Word, explanation, complete silence for ten minutes and then sending them home with three questions; applying the Word to life. The time arrived to spread the experience out to other churches in the city. Seventy priests of the diocese were specially trained to lead the young people in the experience of the Word. Even the unchurched, the ones who claimed that God had no place in their lives, have been reached by letter and by radio. The Word has come alive in that enormous city and diocese.

Very Little Praying

Lots of people regret the disappearance of ways of praying with which they grew up in parish and in school. Some are of the opinion that there is very little praying around today. I would not like to take a bet on that one. It is revealing when you get talking with people, even with the unchurched, to realise that the lifeline to God in their lives never seems to disappear completely. Some people say that they never pray. Maybe, but when they find themselves in the teeth of grave danger the cry 'O God' escapes from their lips. Does the businessman who passes my way almost every day in his huge limousine, in his immaculate suit, his perfectly laundered shirt and smart tie, pray? Many people would automatically conclude that the spiritual world is not part of his agenda. But they are judging him unfairly. He does pray. He told me that he does. As he drives along, particularly when he is held up in traffic he talks, as he says, to 'the man above'. About what? About his business, about those who work with him, about his family, his home and about his parents who live in Spain. A very elementary form of praying perhaps, but praying is very much part of his life. He claims that praying helps him to get things out of his system. He attends Mass on Sundays with his family. I suggested to him that he should take a phrase or a sentence from the readings away with him each week to help him enrich his talking to 'the man above'. Then we got talking about the Bible. After that the prospects are unlimited. A case of an individual who is open to the sacred (2725-2726). John Chrysostom echoes my friend the businessman. 'It is always possible to offer fervent prayer even while walking in public or strolling alone, or seated in your shop ... while buying or selling ... or even while cooking.' (*Ecloga de oratione 2:* PG 63, 585) (2743)

A Great Period
We are living in one of the great periods in history, a period where there is blossoming of prayer and mysticism which can only be compared with sixteenth-century Spain and seventeenth-century France. The fruits of Vatican II are coming alive. The Council went back to what are called the original sources of the Faith. It is now that such sources are bearing fruit. Gradually people are being introduced to the Bible, the liturgy, the early Christian writers. Liturgy exposes people to the best elements in Christian prayer (2652-2662). So do the writings stemming from early Christianity which are so close to the New Testament. People are gradually discovering the great spiritual classics in the western tradition. Through the mutual interchange in the ecumenical movement people are being exposed to the prayer traditions of other Churches. The opening of the Orthodox East to the western Churches has introduced people to incomparable riches. The Charasmatic Movement in its own way has led many to discover prayer and to feel at

home with the Scriptures. The mystics whom we regarded with a degree of suspicion in the past are now being opened up to a wider church. John of the Cross, the great Teresa, Catherine of Siena and Meister Eckhart are no longer the contents lists of unopened books. They are emerging out to a wider Church. The mystics carry with them that touch of God which enkindles desire. The mystics represent the Christian faith at its finest flowering. The mystic is someone who takes God at his word. St Thérèse of the Child Jesus, the centenary of whose death we celebrate in 1997, is a modern mystic who, despite the experience of struggle, darkness and blank wall throughout her life of prayer, remains a concrete example of how trust in God's merciful love can lead to incredible feats of generosity and extraordinary depths of insight into the designs of God. Every age provides its own mystics. Edith Stein, the Jewish philosopher who became a Roman Catholic and later Carmelite nun, stands out in our time as a modern woman who leads us into the depths of finding our whole happiness and peace in God. Edith Stein died in the concentration camp at Auschwitz on 9 August 1942.

Models for Prayer

The Old Testament provides us with amazing models for prayer (2566-2689). The sacrificial praying of Abraham challenges our trust in the divine providence (2570-2573). Moses prays as the mediator for his people (2574-2577). David the King is the outstanding example of a leader who intercedes for his people (2578-2580). Elijah and the prophets stress conversion of heart (2581-2584). The psalms, the prayers of the gathered people of God are expressive of every mood that can arise in the human heart (2585-2588). The psalms are for all the people for all times, for all places (2558-2589). Prayer books by the score have appeared since Vatican II. The vast majority of such collections by enterprising men and women have come and gone. The only stable collection to remain and to be permanently used is the Book of Psalms. The Psalms have been described as the crossroads of the Bible, a kind of super signpost pointing to and absorbing the other books of the Bible. The Psalms are 'the music that never ends'. People are drawn to monasteries by the chanting of the psalms which form a major part of the Divine Office. The Office has been described by St Benedict in his Rule as the work of God (*opus Dei*). The work of God goes on unceasingly.

Female Models
The sections on the Old Testament models of praying are quite substantial in the Catechism. However, the compilers seem to have forgotten the great female models, the prayer and praise of the women of faith, women who were publicly acknowledged as political and religious leaders of the people. Such women have a lot to say to women of our time who are gradually

moving into positions of responsibility and prestige in the society. We think of Judith's passionate prayer and of her song of thanksgiving leading the people in turn to join in her great song (Jdt 9:2-14). Deborah's duet with Barak the son of Abinoan is a magnificent declamation (Jg 5:2-31). The Book of Ruth offers a contrasting model, the quiet and prayerful trust of herself and Naomi. Hannah's jubilant hymn (1 Sam 2:1-10) provides a model, for what has been called the last of the Old Testament Psalms, Mary's Magnificat (Lk 1:46-55). Miriam's song stands out for its booming quality. She leads her people into victory as she plays the tambourine, blaring the refrain which has become familiar to us through the Easter Vigil: 'Sing to the Lord: glorious his triumph, horse and rider he has thrown into the sea' (Ex 15:20). Powerful women all of them, powerful makers of song to the Lord, powerful and life-giving models for the women of our day.

The Prayer of Mary

The pre-eminent model of prayer among women of the Bible is Mary, the Mother of Jesus (2617-2619). St Augustine says she bore the Word in her mind and in her heart before she bore him in her womb. She is the obedient disciple who listens to the Word in faith. That is the way Luke introduces her on to the stage of history in the opening chapter of the Gospel, the woman with a listening ear and a ready heart, in keeping with the spiritual Hebrew tradition of which she is such a shining example. Mary listens. She discerns as she listens to the message of the Gospel (Lk 1:26-38), discerns what God is asking of her. She commits herself in faith when she realises what is being demanded. She then sets out to fulfil the word in action, to minister to her cousin Elizabeth who is to give birth to a son. At the meeting of the two mothers Mary gives expression to the praise of God in the Magnificat, a shout of jubilation which has re-echoed in the Church throughout the centuries.

> The Canticle of Mary, the *Magnificat* (Latin) or *Megalynei* (Byzantine), is the song both of the Mother of God and the Church; the song of the Daughter of Zion and of the new People of God; the song of thanksgiving for the fullness of graces poured out in the economy of salvation and the song of the 'poor' whose hope is met by the fulfilment of the promises made to our ancestors, 'to Abraham and to his posterity forever'. (2619)

The Prayer of Jesus

The prayer of Jesus receives significant coverage in all of the four Gospels, but particularly in the Gospel of Luke. Luke's is *the* Gospel of prayer. He does serve to give us a kind of overview of the prayer of Jesus. Luke's work is saturated in an atmosphere of prayer. To Luke we owe the great canticles which have become so much part of the Church's worship, the

Song of Zechariah, the Benedictus, Mary's Song of the poor, the Magnificat, the Song of the old man Simeon in the Temple and the opening couplet in the Song of the Angels (Gloria in Excelsis Deo), at the birth of Christ. They are the most ancient hymns in our Christian repertoire. They are all of them Jewish Christian songs, exquisitely composed and placed at the lips of the Anawim (God's poor ones). To Luke too we owe the shorter version of the Our Father, the first part of the Hail Mary, most of the Angelus and five joyful mysteries of the Rosary.

Luke is a master of the art of prayer. He describes Jesus at prayer throughout his ministry. Jesus himself instructs at length on how to pray through direct teaching, by means of parable and by drawing the most amazing pictures as in the story of the lepers where the prayer of gratitude is underlined. Every major moment in the life of Christ is filled with prayer.

Luke permeates his writing both in the Gospel and in the Acts of the Apostles with an aura of prayer. Jesus is faithful to the customary times of prayer. His preference seems to be for prayer at night time, often prolonged into the night. 'One of those days Jesus went out in the mountainside to pray and spent the night praying to God' (6:12).

> The Gospel according to St Luke emphasises the action of the Holy Spirit and the meaning of prayer in Christ's ministry. Jesus prays *before* the decisive moments of his mission: before his

Father's witness to him during his baptism and Transfiguration, and before his own fulfilment of the Father's plan of love by his Passion. He also prays before the decisive moments involving the mission of his Apostles: at his election and call of the Twelve, before Peter's confession of him as 'the Christ of God', and again that the faith of the chief of the Apostles may not fail when tempted. Jesus' prayer before the events of salvation that the Father has asked him to fulfil is a humble and trusting commitment of his human will to the will of the Father. (2600)

Gethsemane

Luke narrates the Gethsemane incident in a form somewhat different from the other two Synoptic Gospels. Obviously the disciples knew the place, a definite locale. Jesus had often prayed there through the watches of the night. This incident is in itself a whole catechesis on prayer. Jesus accepts the steadfast will of the Father as opposed to what could be his own fickle desire. All genuine praying must in the end lead to acceptance of the will of the Father. Genuine prayer will include both discernment and decision, the outcome of the gift of consolation which comes from the Spirit. (2749)

There is almost an anxiety on the part of Jesus to be faithful to the will of the Father which runs like a refrain through his life and prayer, beginning with the incident in the Temple following the boy's loss. Jesus is able to be in solitude, alone with the Father, and is able to be with people at the same time. He seems to be able to reach out to the Father and to people with equal ease.

Praying in Us
Jesus not only prays to the Father, not only includes all men and women in his prayer as the Incarnate Word taking our flesh upon himself, but empowers the prayer of all Christians. In the end it is not we who do the praying but Christ who prays in us.

St Augustine summarises wonderfully the three dimensions of Jesus' prayer: 'He prays for us as our priest, prays in us as our head, and is prayed to by us as our God therefore let us acknowledge our voice in him and his in us' (2616). St Paul's theology of the Christian at prayer is summed up in one very powerful line in the letter to the Galatians '…the proof that you are sons is that God has sent the Spirit of his Son into our hearts, the Spirit that cries *"Abba Father"* ' (4:6). Abba, an Aramaic word, the mother tongue of Jesus, is the intimate expression of a child calling its father Papa or Daddy. We stand in Christ's own relationship to the Father and to the Spirit who prompts our praying. A most important section of the Catechism tells us that prayer is Trinitarian: we pray to the Father, through the Son and in the Holy Spirit. This is the classical liturgical approach to prayer. All Christian praying is the 'love of God which has been poured into our hearts by the Holy Spirit' (Rm 5:5). That single sentence is probably the most total description of prayer that we could possibly think of. Prayer is the love which already exists in the Christian heart coming alive.

Praying in the Heart

The heart is the shorthand which has been employed for the living presence of the Spirit within us, by means of which we pray. The heart is a term to be found in the Old Testament and in the New. It is taken up by the early Christian writers and by the monks of the Eastern Desert to describe the innermost part of one's being. What the French call 'le cime de l'esprit'. It has been translated as the peak of the spirit, the core of the personality, the deepest layer of the self, what Carl Rogers calls 'the innermost self'.

It is in the innermost self within the heart that prayer is born. With most people the heart is asleep and surfaces to consciousness only very rarely in an age which promotes transistorised noise and confusion. The main enterprise in prayer is to discover the way into one's own heart, into that unknown inner region which many discern as the source of health and harmony. The task of praying is to discover what Peter calls 'the hidden man of the heart' (1 P 3:4). The heart is already in a state of prayer. Prayer is something already received with the gift of Baptism. Prayer is the heart's awakening to love. (2652-2653)

Gathering Up
In a beautiful passage, the Catechism comments on the biblical meaning of the heart. 'The heart is the dwelling place, where I am, where I live…' (2562) our hidden centre, beyond the grasp of our reason and of others; only the Spirit of God can fathom the human heart and know it fully.

The heart is the place of decision, deeper than our psychic drives. It is the place of faith, where we choose life or death. It is the place of encounter, because as image of God we live in relation: it is the place of covenant (2563). 'Entering into contemplative prayer is like entering into the Eucharistic liturgy; we "gather up" the heart, recollect our whole being under the prompting of the Holy Spirit.... We let our masks fall and turn our hearts back to the Lord who loves us so as to hand ourselves over to be purified and transformed'. (2711)

The Life of Prayer
In the Catholic church we sometimes use the phrase 'life of prayer'. Prayer, like life, has different movements, different moments of growth and decline. It has rhythms, prayer in the morning and in the evening. Sunday is the great day for prayer and for the celebration of the Eucharist. The liturgical year gives a fundamental rhythm to prayer. (2697-2699)

Prayer can be described as a tuning in to God. The Christian who endeavours to be a Christian in daily life is always tuned to God. One's whole life becomes 'a living sacrifice of praise' (Eucharistic Prayer III). The living sacrifice of praise is lived out in the day-to-day events of life. We encounter God in such events when we say yes to what they demand of us. Saying yes all the time is not easy, saying yes to life, to people and to society, to the downs of life as well as the ups. Such responsible activity in daily life can be described as Gospel maturity. It is prayer in the broad sense. It becomes praying all of the time everywhere. Praying all of the time everywhere demands equally that we pray some of the time somewhere, that we find a time and a place to show the true face of our selves to the Lord, to purify the yes that we make to life, to people and to society. (2660-2710)

Times of Prayer

The time we will spend on personal prayer, heart-to-heart communing with the Lord, will depend very much on our other commitments in life. (2727) There seems to be a great deal of unanimity among the great world religions on the early morning as a suitable time for praying. In the early morning our minds are comparatively still, not yet besieged by the thousand and one demands that meet us once the day progresses. The beginning of a new day suggests power, the beginning of new life, fresh energy. New life for the world of nature waking from its sleep. New life for one who is ready to receive it in the outpouring of self in the presence of one's God. If one does not have the time for solitary prayer at the beginning of the day the following little formula from the Russian tradition is to be recommended. The author is one Philaret of Moscow.

> O Lord grant me to greet this coming day in peace. Help me in all things to rely on your holy will. In every hour of the day reveal your holy will to me. Bless my dealings with all who surround me. Teach me to treat all that comes to me throughout the day with peace of soul, and with the firm conviction that your will governs all. In all my deeds and words, guide my thoughts and feelings. In unforeseen events let me not forget that all are sent by you. Teach me to act firmly and wisely, without embittering and embarrassing others. Give me the strength to bear the fatigue of the coming day with all that it shall bring. Direct my will; teach me to pray; pray in me.

The Sunset Hour

If one cannot find the time to pray in the early morning the next most relaxed and opportune time seems to be the evening, according to many of the leading religious systems. At the sunset hour things begin to calm down. The majority of people who work what are called social hours are on their way home from work. Families come together after the day's work.

The family evening meal must be one of the most privileged times of the day. I am reminded of the distinction which one scripture scholar made concerning the Eucharist in New Testament. He distinguished the Eucharist with a big 'E' from the Eucharist with a small 'e', the Eucharist at the altar from the eucharist around the family table. At the family evening meal there can be a very relaxed atmosphere which gives the family an opportunity to share. I have been told by parents that it can be a time when everything is capable of being told, who said what to whom during the day, who misbehaved and who was funny. A family should take advantage of such a privileged moment to prolong the meal, to talk and perhaps to pray. In a family of eight children in a suburban area of Dublin the end of the meal was the occasion to ask who or what should be prayed for this evening? Family prayer in the Roman Catholic situation has fallen into disuse in recent times. Fractured lives, varied engagements and television all tend to make inroads on family life. We still have to re-invent family ritual prayer. (2685)

The Place for Prayer
The place we choose for prayer can be of considerable help. If we can find a place that is well-ordered, clean, quiet and free from distractions, we have already established the conditions in which personal heart-to-heart communion is more easily attained. We have to realise that nowadays such space can be a lux-

ury. The arm of God's grace, though, is never shortened by our circumstances in life. An overriding rule was stated long ago by a down-to-earth English Benedictine monk, Dom John Chapman: 'Pray as you can, not as you can't'. Some of the purest forms of prayer arise not from the ideal time or place, but from our experience in life. (2691)

Witness

Another factor which helps enormously is the witness of a believing community. This witness used to be present in parishes in days gone by in the shape of associations like sodalities and confraternities which gave a human support to our life of faith. Today the small group has taken over in various forms, such as the prayer group, groups that come together for Bible study, *Lectio Divina,* family support, cells, liturgy preparation groups, etc. Well over a half a century ago the German theologian Romano Guardini, whose writings had such an impact on Vatican II, uttered a statement which at the time seemed radical but is taken for granted in our time. 'The reason for the diminished faith and a diminished implementation of the faith is basically our unwillingness or our inability to share our faith experience with each other'.

Communion

Having chosen the time and place for prayer the next step is to enter communion with mystery because that is what prayer is all about, a coming into contact with something greater than myself in order to become my true self. It is a coming into contact, a communion with a presence which is, paradoxically, above me, beyond me, far away from me and, at the same time, is within me, nearer to me than breathing.

Conviction about the need for prayer in my life will lead to a determination to enter into contact with that presence each day – that presence which is ever leading me on towards deeds of unselfishness, and dedication of myself. To fail to respond to this presence is a great pity because in the end it involves a failure to become myself. We all unfortunately succumb to the demanding pressures that are at work in our lives. It is the easiest thing in the world to find excuses not to pray. There are some people who are so attuned to this presence that they carry about with them the memory of it all the time. For most people it takes a deliberate effort to find time for the celebration of this daily sacrament, for communion with mystery, the presence within. I give my own definition of prayer for what it is worth: 'an entering into communion with that other who enables me to become my true self'. God is the ground of my being. Eckhart stated that 'my me is God'. My me is that inner part of me where I discover his living presence, what Catherine of Siena calls the interior cell. (2565)

Ways of Praying

How do I pray? This is the plea that arises from many a heart, from people looking for someone to show them the way. So often I hear the complaint, 'I would love to be able to pray. Somehow I never seem to get round to it. I never seem to get the time.' I sometimes ask such people, 'Have you ever thought of the Jesus Prayer?' Many people will never have heard of it. The Jesus Prayer is a prayer for all seasons, for the experienced as well as for the beginner. The usual formula is 'Jesus Christ, Son of God, Saviour, have mercy on me, a sinner'. There is free use of it as opposed to the formal use of it. The free use of it is compatible with the normal daily tasks. As Bishop Theophon puts it: 'the hands at work, the mind and heart with God'. In the formal use of the prayer the whole attention is concentrated on the saying of it, to the exclusion of everything else. It combines adoration with repentance, ascent with descent, breathing out with breathing in. By constant repetition of the name we bear the presence of Christ within us. The Jesus Prayer is Trinitarian as well as Christological and contains within itself the whole Gospel truth. It is the subject of a lovely book born out of the Russian tradition, *The Way of a Pilgrim,* which reads like a travel book. The Jesus Prayer is a way of fulfilling the New Testament injunction to pray always. (2616, 2667-68)

Lectio Divina

One could devote a whole book to this way of praying, possibly the oldest way of praying in the Church. Lectio finds its origin in the Scriptures and is systematised in the Rule of St Benedict in the sixth century. Lectio in our time has become a widespread movement of 'rediscovery and appropriation of the Bible by the people' (Carlos Mesters). Lectio combines the twin expressions of prayer emphasised by the Catechism, meditation and contemplative prayer. Cardinal Martini translates the age-old term 'Lectio Divina' as a spiritual reading of the Bible. Lectio goes from reading to pondering to conversation to resting with the Word. The reading becomes more an appropriation of a biblical text. One ruminates on it, allowing it to echo and re-echo inside oneself, to become acquainted with each detail and to wrestle with its demands on one's life (1177, 2708). Cardinal Martini sums it up this way: 'I am convinced that for a Christian today, it is difficult, if not impossible, to keep one's faith without nourishing oneself through listening to Scripture personally as well as with others. In this way a believer learns to rest in the heart of God and one trains oneself to look at people and their weaknesses with the eyes of God.'

Centering Prayer

Centering prayer is rooted in the Word of God as it has a close connection with the practice of Lectio Divina. This way of prayer is an effort to renew the Christian contemplative tradition which goes back to St Paul who wrote of an intimate knowledge of Christ through faith and love (cf. Eph 3:14-19). The method itself is based on the teaching contained in the fourteenth-century English classic, *The Cloud of Unknowing*. The heart and soul of centering prayer is the intention to consent to the presence and action of God in one's life.

This intention is expressed and symbolised by the use of a single word of one or two syllables, called the sacred word, chosen by the person praying, to gently draw the attention back to God whenever one becomes aware of any kind of distraction. It is not used constantly but only when necessary to reaffirm one's intention to be in God's presence and to submit to God's purifying action in one's life. This sacred word symbolises the movement of the will to consent to God's presence and action within. We need do nothing more; we simply trust that God will accept our intention and make it bear fruit.

The Liturgy of the Hours

The Liturgy of the Hours, otherwise called the Prayer of the Church or the Divine Office, is an institution that refuses to die. Increasingly, lay people across the world are being acquainted with Hours. The Basic Christian Communities of Brazil have their own adapted version. In France a monthly disposable prayer book, *Magnificat,* gives the texts for the daily Mass readings, for Morning Prayer, Evening Prayer and Compline. The injunction to pray constantly (1 Th 5:17; Eph 6:18) finds expression in the Liturgy of the Hours which is so devised that the whole course of the day and the night is made holy by the praise of God. The Hours become sacramental entry points into the mystery of Christ. The General Instruction on the Liturgy of the Hours which introduces the 1970 edition of the Roman Breviary has been regarded as the finest document promulgated by the teaching Church on prayer. The Instruction brings out the fuller pastoral nature of the Liturgy of the Hours. The Hours belong to the very essence of the Church itself which is a community and which in prayer must express itself as a community. There is no conflict between the Hours and personal prayer. One gives vitality to the other. I would love to see the Hours extended to the whole Church. To attain such a goal maybe further adaptation is needed.

The Rosary
The Rosary, like the Angelus, derives from the Liturgy of the Hours. It used to be called the layman's breviary. The Rosary beads in the Roman Catholic tradition is akin to the prayer rope of the Eastern Churches. Having something in the hands to count with while saying a form of vocal prayer fosters a contemplative way of praying. Older persons confined to their homes saying Rosary after Rosary tend to be real contempla-

tives. Such persons are at the heart of the praying Church. Carlo Caretto of the Little Brothers of Jesus claims that he had to go into the desert to learn how to say the Rosary. (1174-1178)

Conclusion – The Lord's Prayer

'Jesus was praying in a certain place and when he had ceased one of his disciples said to him – "Lord, teach us to pray"' (Lk 11:1). 'By contemplating the master prayer the children learn to pray to the Father' (2601). The prayer which Jesus taught to his disciples is the prayer of Christian identity. It suggests both a way of praying and a way of living. The Lord's Prayer is, according to Tertullian, a summary of the entire Gospel (2761). The Catechism ends with an entire commentary on the Lord's Prayer. This is in keeping with a very ancient tradition. Most of the patristic commentaries on the Our Father are addressed to catechumens and neophytes. The handing on of the tradition of the Lord's Prayer in Baptism and Confirmation signifies new birth into the divine life. (2769)

> The Sermon on the Mount is teaching for life, the *Our Father* is a prayer; but in both the one and the other the Spirit gives new form to our desires those inner movements that animate our lives. Jesus teaches us this new life by his words; he teaches us to ask for it by our prayer. The rightness of our life in him will depend on the rightness of our prayer. (2764)